Taking a Bath in Rome

Erin Ash Sullivan

Newbridge
A Haights Cross Communications ®️ Company

BEFORE YOU READ

Imagine having to fetch water from a well just to take a bath! That's what ancient Romans had to do. Or, at least they did until Rome became so crowded that they had to find a better way of getting water. What solutions do you think they came up with? As you get ready to read this book, think about the following and make notes.

What do you know about life in ancient Rome? Where have you read about or seen pictures of Roman aqueducts, fountains, and baths?

The Romans believed it was important to keep clean. Why do you think this was so?

Preview the book by looking at the table of contents, headings, photos, and special features.

What do you see in this book that you already know something about?

List three facts or ideas you think you'll discover in this book.

Look at the quotation in the "Talk of the Town" box on page 9. What do the words of Vitruvius tell you about the water supply in ancient Rome?

Write down two questions you have about the Romans' early plumbing and how it affected life in ancient Rome.

CONTENTS

WASHING AWAY THE DAY

I t's been a long, busy day. You're looking forward to a little down time. So, you walk into a large building and wave to a few friends as you pass by. You head to the gym for a refreshing workout. Perhaps you'll run a few laps around a track. Then, it's off to the steam room, followed by a dip in the pool. Before you head home, you stop at the library and chat with friends. This may sound like modern-day America to you. But it's not. Actually, we're talking about an afternoon in ancient Rome.

The ancient Romans were thinkers, writers, and scientists—but mostly they were warriors. From 264 BC on, Roman soldiers traveled around the world to conquer other lands. They marched across Europe, sailed over the Mediterranean Sea, and created a huge **empire.** At one point, this empire stretched from England to northern Africa.

▼ Ancient Rome was a thriving **metropolis** and the capital of the Roman Empire. Located near the western coast of Italy, it is now that country's capital.

Wherever the Romans went, they built towns and brought their culture and ideas to other groups of people.

At the time, the Roman Empire was the most powerful state in the world, with the city of Rome at its center. The Romans built impressive public buildings. They constructed roads in and out of the city, so their armies could march from one place to another. And they created laws to keep the city running smoothly. Throughout the city, you could find art galleries, theaters, and restaurants.

At its peak, the city of Rome had more than one million residents. With a population that big, the Romans ran into some serious challenges. One of them was finding enough water for everyone. This was a big problem that required big solutions.

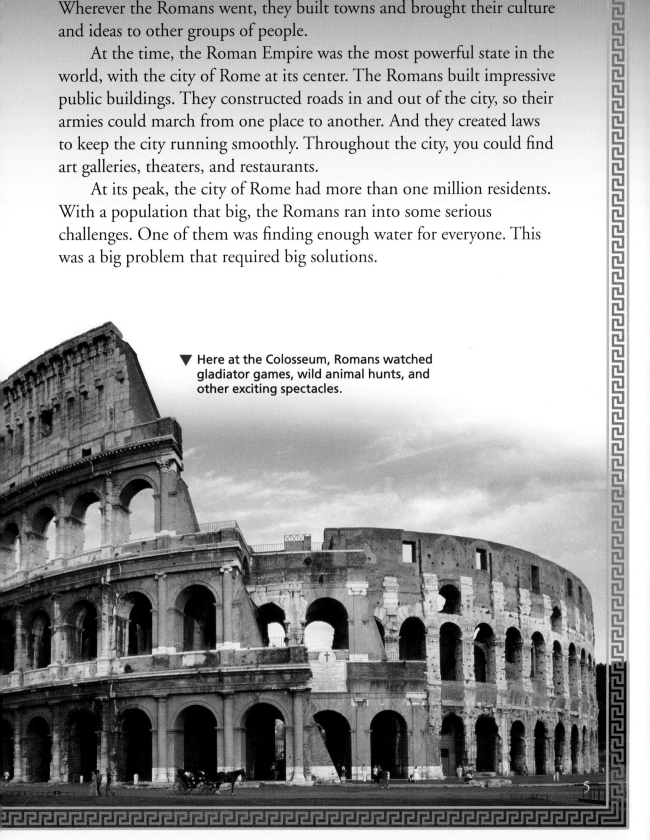

▼ Here at the Colosseum, Romans watched gladiator games, wild animal hunts, and other exciting spectacles.

Big City, Big Problem

Ancient Rome was a crowded, noisy city. It bustled with activity, as people went about their daily lives. Some Romans were wealthy and powerful. But most were laborers who earned small wages. Many others were slaves. Wherever they went, Roman soldiers brought back slaves from the lands that they conquered.

Rich or poor, all of Rome's residents needed water for drinking, cooking, and washing. They also needed a way to go to the bathroom and get rid of waste. Without a good supply of clean water, sickness could spread easily.

The Romans believed that staying clean was extremely important. Was it because they didn't like the idea of being around sweaty, smelly people? Maybe. More important, though, they knew that people had to be clean to be healthy. And the Roman Empire needed healthy soldiers to keep its army strong and to conquer other lands.

As more and more people poured into Rome, the city leaders knew they had a big problem on their hands. How could they get clean, fresh water to so many people?

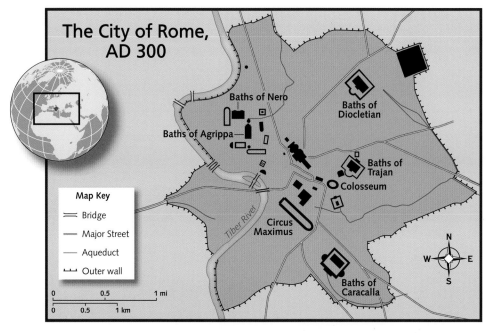

▲ At that time, Rome was surrounded by a wall for protection. The city had several public buildings including stadiums and **baths**.

The Romans were excellent problem solvers. Their city's planners came up with several solutions. It took the work of builders and plumbers to put these solutions into action. **Channels,** or waterways, were constructed to bring in water from miles away. Underground pipes created by plumbers sent the water throughout the city. Beautiful stone fountains provided fresh water for drinking and cooking. Public baths kept Romans clean and healthy. And sewers and public toilets took care of all the waste.

Why should anyone today care about pipes and **sewers** in ancient Rome? Believe it or not, plumbing can tell you a lot about how people lived long ago. For example, it can show you how they bathed, cooked, and cleaned. It can also show differences between how rich and poor people lived.

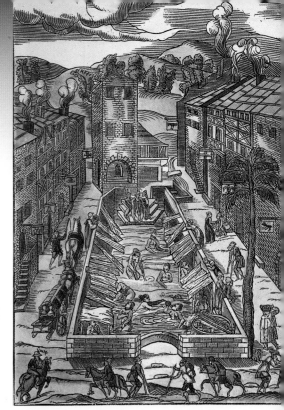

▲ This painting from the 1600s shows what it might have been like to take a bath in ancient Rome. Back then, people didn't mind bathing together.

▼ Rich Romans lived in grand homes. Poor people lived in cramped apartments. A modern-day architect created this model to show a typical Roman apartment building. Entire families were often crowded into one room with no running water.

ALONG THE AQUEDUCTS

The year is AD 115. You're traveling from a place called Britannia (a place that will later be known as Great Britain), on your way to Rome. You've heard it's the greatest city in the world, and you can't wait to see it for the first time. In a valley outside the city, you notice an incredible sight. In the distance stands one of Rome's most famous structures—the Aqua Claudia. It looks something like a bridge, but it's not. It's an **aqueduct** that's designed to carry water into the city. Wealthy Romans have built country homes in this valley so they can take in the breathtaking view. But aqueducts are more than just pretty sights. They're Rome's water lifelines.

◀ Early waterways were narrow channels dug into the ground and lined with stones. This one leads to an ancient fort.

The first step to solving the water problem was finding a way to bring enough of it into the city. The Romans' solution was to build aqueducts. These incredible waterways were made to carry water over great distances into Rome.

Over a period of about 500 years, from 312 BC to AD 226, the Romans built 11 aqueducts. These waterways carried enough water to supply about 200 gallons a day for each person in the city. That's a lot of water. Especially if you consider the fact that most Americans today use about 100 gallons of water a day.

TALK OF THE TOWN

How to Find Water

How could you find a good source of water in ancient Rome? Take the advice of Vitruvius, an architect who lived there. "Before sunrise, lie face-down on the ground with your chin on your hands. Look over the countryside. Where you see vapor curling up from the ground, you will find water where you dig."

▼ The Aqua Claudia aqueduct took 14 years to build and was completed in AD 50. It was named after Claudius, who was **emperor** at the time.

9

Building an Aqueduct

Before they could begin building, the Romans had to find a source of water. It couldn't be too far away. Anything more than 60 miles or so just wouldn't work. Then, there was the Romans' good taste to consider. They liked the taste of fresh water from mountain springs. Actually, they weren't too different from a lot of people today. Think of all the bottles of spring water that line store shelves.

After careful thought, the Romans decided to go to the Apennine Mountains. The water there tasted good and it wasn't too far away.

Once the Romans found water, the hard work began. It took several years to build a single aqueduct. And the construction was extremely difficult. Ancient Romans didn't have forklifts, cranes, or other machines that we have today. Plus, the project was expensive,

Italy's Mountains

▲ Italy is also known as the Apennine Peninsula after the mountain range that stretches across most of the country.

took a long time, and required careful planning. And imagine all the workers it took to build just one aqueduct. Slaves, poor laborers, and soldiers all had to work together.

To see how the aqueducts worked, take a simple straw. Tilt it at a slight angle, and carefully pour water into the higher end. What does the water do? It runs downward through the straw and comes out the other end. The water rolls downward for one reason—**gravity.**

The aqueducts were built with the same idea in mind. Roman **engineers** used the power of gravity to move water from one place to another. They built the aqueducts on a gradual slope, or slant, even if the ground itself was level. That way, the water would roll along on its own.

◄ Ancient aqueducts were constructed out of stone and often had pipes made of lead or clay. Today, we use materials such as steel, like these tubes, to build modern waterways.

▼ The Apennines stretch 870 miles. This mountain range has forested slopes and fresh mountain springs.

Tunnels and Arches

Using gravity to move water made a lot of sense. But that method also required clever planning and designing. The Romans needed long aqueducts that would carry water from the mountains all the way into the city. They had to build them very tall and with a slope that was very gradual. If it wasn't tall enough or if the slope was too steep, the aqueduct would be pretty short. That's because it would run only a couple of miles or so before it touched the ground.

That wasn't the only challenge. Hills and valleys also covered the countryside. It was difficult to build aqueducts with mountains in the way. To solve that problem, workers dug tunnels through the hills. In fact, most of Rome's aqueducts ran underground for part of the way.

When the aqueducts ran above ground, they were held up by curved **arches.** The arches were strong and could support the weight of the waterway. Arches were attractive, too. The Romans believed

▼ This painting shows ancient Roman ruins as they appeared in the 1800s. The city of Rome was built on seven hills. Imagine trying to construct aqueducts around that.

that **architecture** should be beautiful as well as useful. And Rome's aqueducts were truly beautiful, with arches gracefully stretching across the landscape.

So spring water from the Apennines flowed along aqueducts, through mountains, over valleys, and eventually made its way into Rome. By the time the water reached the city, it was pretty clean. That's because the water passed through tanks that **filtered,** or sifted, out dirt at certain spots along the way. Also, the aqueducts weren't completely covered. That meant air came in contact with the water, which also helped keep it fresh and clean. Once inside the city, the water was stored in gigantic containers.

Shutting Down the Supply

The Roman Empire began to weaken in the 500s. Invaders in the north, who were known as **barbarians,** attacked the city and took control. They destroyed almost all of the aqueducts, cutting off the city's water supply. By the time they were done, the only aqueduct that still worked was the Aqua Virgo, which ran completely underground. For centuries after, no one used aqueducts. People returned to the old ways. They got their water supply straight from rivers and wells.

▼ Many historians believe that the Romans were the best ancient aqueduct builders. But the Egyptians and Babylonians built them, too.

13

WATER, WATER, EVERYWHERE

The first thing you notice as you enter the ancient city of Rome are all the fountains. You're surprised by how many there are. As far as you can tell, most Romans are a few steps away from fresh drinking water. You pass the **Baths** of Trajan. This elaborate structure was built by the emperor as a gift to the city a few years back. People stream in and out of this famous bathhouse. Back home in Britannia, people would find the baths awfully strange. To you, Rome is truly a city of wonders.

◀ Rich people in the Roman Empire could afford to build fountains for their homes, like the one shown here.

▲ One of Rome's most famous landmarks, the Trevi Fountain, was built between 1732 and 1762. In ancient times, this spot marked the end point of the Aqua Virgo aqueduct.

One of the great things about the Roman plumbing system was that everyone could get clean, fresh water. Rich and poor alike. Many water pipes carried water to public fountains. That's where common people got their water for drinking and cooking. A bucket or two could be pretty heavy. So Romans were happy to have fountains close to their homes. Then they wouldn't have to carry their water so far.

The richest people had pipes leading directly into their homes. Having plumbing in your own house was a luxury and you were charged according to the size of the pipe. The bigger the pipe, the bigger the water bill. If the water level decreased during dry spells, private homes would be the first to lose their supply. Public fountains would be the last.

Pompeii was a city located south of Rome that was part of the Roman Empire. Many homes were no more than a few hundred feet from a fountain. That made fetching water an easy job.

Pipes and Plumbers

If you could peek beneath the streets of ancient Rome, you'd find a maze of lead pipes. They stretched throughout the city. Rome's underground system was a lot like the plumbing we have today. Except, there was one big difference: Today's pipes have **valves**. You can shut them off and stop the water from flowing. Most Roman pipes had no valves. That meant water ran through them all the time.

Who looked after all those pipes? Plumbers. In fact, the word "plumber" comes from *plumbum*, which means "lead" in Latin, the language that Romans spoke. "Plumber" was a good name for these workers because they built and repaired pipes made of lead.

◀ Some Roman pipes were made out of wood or clay. But most were made of lead.

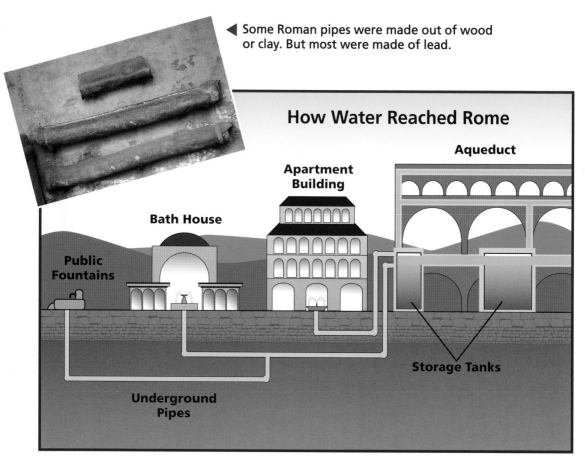

How Water Reached Rome

Aqueduct

Apartment Building

Bath House

Public Fountains

Storage Tanks

Underground Pipes

▲ Water traveled along aqueducts that ended just inside the city. There, the water was kept in tanks and sent through pipes to homes, bathhouses, and fountains.

Plumbers also connected the pipes to the water supply. The lead used to make them was usually mined in the country now called Spain. It was then shipped to Rome.

Roman plumbers were laborers who worked long hours for little pay. But they were important. Without them, the city of Rome wouldn't have been nearly as clean. Their work was needed in ancient times, just as it is in the modern world.

▼ Today's plumbers not only repair pipes, they also fix faucets, set up water heaters, and install garbage disposals.

Into the Sewers

Just picture it. All that water, flowing through pipes. It shoots out of fountains. It fills up the baths. And it flushes away waste. But, we'll get to that part of the story later.

Romans used a lot of water. And when they were done with it, it had to go somewhere. Keep in mind that most Roman pipes had no valves. Water flowed through them all the time. So where did it all go?

As you know, Romans built channels to bring in water. They also built channels to carry it out. These channels were called sewers. They were connected to public buildings like the baths. They also went into the homes of wealthy people. The sewers carried excess water and waste out of the city, and dumped it into the nearby Tiber River.

There was a major problem with the sewers, though—the bad odor. There were few valves to close off the pipes. So the smell from the sewers often traveled back up the pipes. As a result, ancient Roman toilets smelled pretty bad. And that wasn't the only problem. Although the sewers did an important job, they caused terrible pollution in the Tiber River.

▼ This sewer is called the Cloaca Maxima. That means "greatest drain" in Latin. It was the largest and oldest sewer in ancient Rome.

Then there was the flooding. A Roman named Pliny wrote, "Sometimes, the backwash of the Tiber floods the sewers and makes its way along them upstream." Imagine dirty floodwater coming up through the pipes into the city streets. The dirty sewers were breeding grounds for germs and were the cause of much illness throughout Rome.

But even with these problems, the sewer system still helped Romans get rid of waste water filled with dirt and germs. The most impressive part of the system was called the Cloaca Maxima. This huge channel was built in the sixth century BC. It was made to carry away water during storms. Eventually, it became part of the sewer system. Parts of it are still used today. In fact, you could tour some of this ancient landmark on a trip to Rome.

▼ Sewers still form a network beneath towns and cities. But today, they're linked to treatment plants. Those are facilities that handle waste so that it doesn't pollute the environment.

AN AFTERNOON AT THE BATHS

During your visit to ancient Rome, you need to take care of a couple of important things. You've got to clean up and find a place to use the toilet. Luckily for you, a Roman bathhouse is nearby. You look forward to spending a few hours there, knowing that you'll leave feeling clean and refreshed.

The Romans loved their aqueducts and their sewers. But they loved their baths even more because they believed that staying clean and healthy was very important. But most Romans didn't have running water in their homes. So over the years, several of Rome's emperors paid for bathhouses to be built. They wanted to make sure that just about everyone—including the poorest workers—would be able to get clean on a daily basis. Most bathhouses were massive buildings with many rooms. Building them was complicated and cost an enormous amount of money.

Some bathhouses were huge. They covered several city blocks, like today's malls. ▶

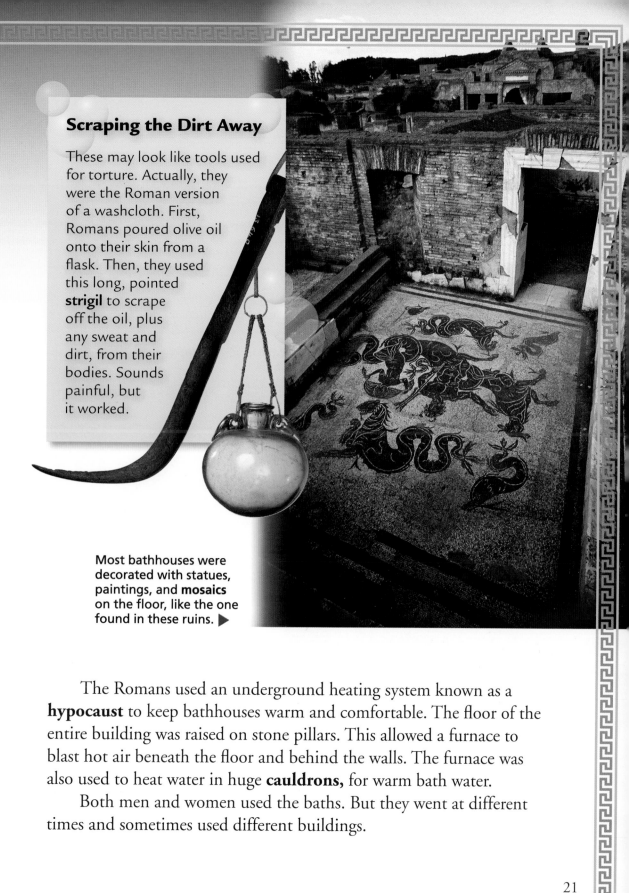

Scraping the Dirt Away

These may look like tools used for torture. Actually, they were the Roman version of a washcloth. First, Romans poured olive oil onto their skin from a flask. Then, they used this long, pointed **strigil** to scrape off the oil, plus any sweat and dirt, from their bodies. Sounds painful, but it worked.

Most bathhouses were decorated with statues, paintings, and **mosaics** on the floor, like the one found in these ruins. ▶

The Romans used an underground heating system known as a **hypocaust** to keep bathhouses warm and comfortable. The floor of the entire building was raised on stone pillars. This allowed a furnace to blast hot air beneath the floor and behind the walls. The furnace was also used to heat water in huge **cauldrons,** for warm bath water.

Both men and women used the baths. But they went at different times and sometimes used different buildings.

Bathtime!

The Romans made it cheap to be clean. They kept bathhouse prices low, and children could enter for free. Plus, there were plenty of places to go, with thousands of bathhouses across the Roman Empire. The biggest could hold more than 1,500 people. That made bathing easy for almost everyone. But taking a bath in ancient Rome wasn't just a quick scrub behind the ears. It was a long process with many steps. So let's see what it was like to take a bath, Roman style. *Bene lave!* That's Latin for "Have a good bath!"

▼ These are the remains of the Baths of Caracalla, one of Rome's most famous bathhouses. It was built by Emperor Caracalla, who reigned from AD 211 to 217.

Emperor Caracalla

TAKING A ROMAN BATH, STEP-BY-STEP

Step 1
Drop your clothes in the *apodyterium*. Don't worry about anyone trying to steal them. You can pay an attendant to watch them for you.

Step 2
Stop in the *palaestra* for a little exercise. You can work out with weights or wrestle with a friend.

Step 3
Time for the *caldarium,* the hottest room of the baths. You'll need wooden sandals to protect your feet from the hot floor.

Step 4
Next, you can head to a warm room called a *tepidarium*. A paid servant will use a strigil to scrape oil and dirt off your skin.

Step 5
The *frigidarium* is the coldest of the rooms. Jump into the pool fast, if you want to get a shock to your system.

Step 6
Last but not least, take a swim in the *natatorium,* or swimming pool, to feel refreshed and relaxed!

Not Just a Bath... an Adventure!

A Roman bath wasn't just for getting clean. It was also a great place to get together with friends, relax, and have fun. Besides rooms for bathing, there were libraries for reading. There were also rooms for massages and spa treatments. If you had time, you could stroll through mini-museums filled with paintings and statues. People could visit shops and cafés near the entrance, too.

So let's say that you haven't seen your friend Marcus in a while. The two of you can arrange to meet at the baths in the early afternoon.

▲ The Romans passed hot steam through holes or hollow tiles in the walls to heat the caldarium. Hot water was also carried from the furnace and poured into basins and pools.

Washbowls like this one have been found in old Roman baths. ▶

While you're running on the track or dunking in the pools, you can catch up on the news. You'll definitely hear all the latest gossip. Afterwards you can wander by paintings in the art gallery. Or you might admire a few statues. Before you know it, three hours have gone by.

For many Romans, taking a bath was the best part of the day. Wealthy citizens might have baths in their homes, but most still went to public bathhouses regularly. No wonder, when it was so much fun.

TALK OF THE TOWN

Bad Neighbors

Poor Seneca. He was a Roman writer and philosopher who lived in an apartment above a busy bathhouse. He wrote, "Picture to yourself now the assortment of voices, the sound of which is enough to make you sick. When the stronger fellows are exercising and swinging heavy weights in their hands, when they are working hard, or pretending to be working hard, I hear their groans; and whenever they release their pent-up breath, I hear their hissing and jarring breathing...."

▼ It's still a good idea to work up a healthy sweat. It clears out your skin and helps keep dirt from clogging your pores.

When You Gotta Go...

Now we've come to a topic that people don't talk much about because it's embarrassing—toilets. But it's still useful to know how ancient Romans handled going to the toilet. Without a way to safely get rid of waste, people can't stay healthy.

Many Romans used the public toilets. You could find them at the baths or in other public places. Public toilets were large rooms with stone benches placed along opposite walls. The benches had holes cut in them where people could sit down and take care of business. Water from the aqueducts rushed beneath the benches. It carried the waste away into the sewers.

▼ This **latrine** was found in Tunisia, which was once part of the Roman Empire. Twelve people could use it at once.

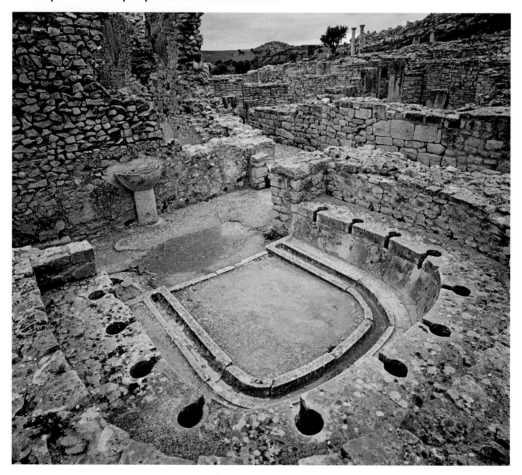

Many people used the toilet at the same time. And men and women used the same facilities. People often took their time to chat with neighbors. But conversation wasn't the only thing the ancient Romans shared. They also shared the ancient Roman version of toilet paper. It was a sponge tied to a stick. When you finished with the sponge stick, you placed it in a container of salt water to clean it. It was then ready for the next person.

If you needed to use the toilet in your own home, you might go straight to the kitchen. Not every Roman lived in a home with a kitchen, but the ones that did usually had holes in the kitchen floors covered with seats and used as toilets. The kitchen was often the only room with pipes connected to the sewer. Plus, the Romans could pour used water from cooking pots into the toilet to flush away the waste.

But some people didn't have pipes in their homes at all. That was especially true if they lived on the upper floors of apartment buildings. In that case, they would use a pot and empty it out the window at night. This was a good reason to stay off the streets of Rome after dark. You never knew what might land on your head.

▼ Imagine heading into your kitchen to use the toilet—many Romans did!

ACROSS THE ROMAN EMPIRE

I t's now AD 120, several years after your trip to the city of Rome. You still remember all the amazing sights and sounds that you experienced. The aqueducts and bathhouses stand out in particular. Both of those have already been built near you in the countryside of Britannia. As the Roman Empire spread to the far corners of the world, so did the Romans' good ideas. This meant that thousands of miles from Rome, you could find Roman roads, Roman buildings, and Roman plumbing.

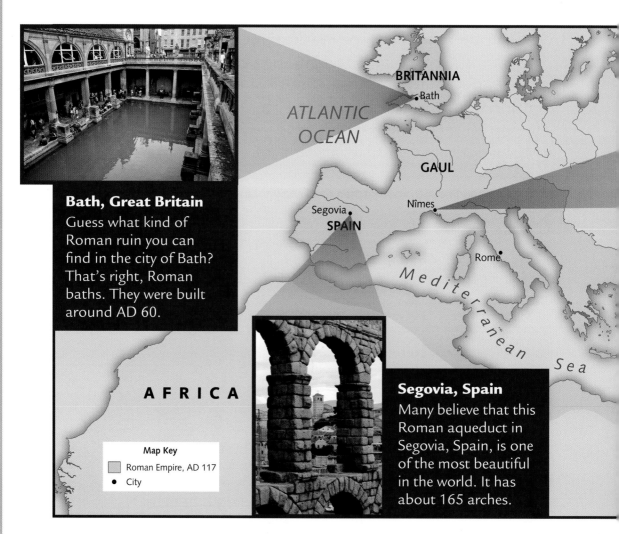

Bath, Great Britain
Guess what kind of Roman ruin you can find in the city of Bath? That's right, Roman baths. They were built around AD 60.

BRITANNIA
• Bath

ATLANTIC OCEAN

GAUL

Segovia •
SPAIN

Nîmes •

Rome •

Mediterranean Sea

AFRICA

Map Key
☐ Roman Empire, AD 117
• City

Segovia, Spain
Many believe that this Roman aqueduct in Segovia, Spain, is one of the most beautiful in the world. It has about 165 arches.

While the Roman Empire was strong and healthy, its armies conquered countries around the world. Whenever the Romans took control of an area, they put their own government systems in place. The leaders also planned cities using the same solutions that worked in Rome. That meant cities around the world got their own aqueducts, baths, and sewers. Even after the Roman Empire fell from power, the Romans' good ideas lived on. Take a look and see for yourself.

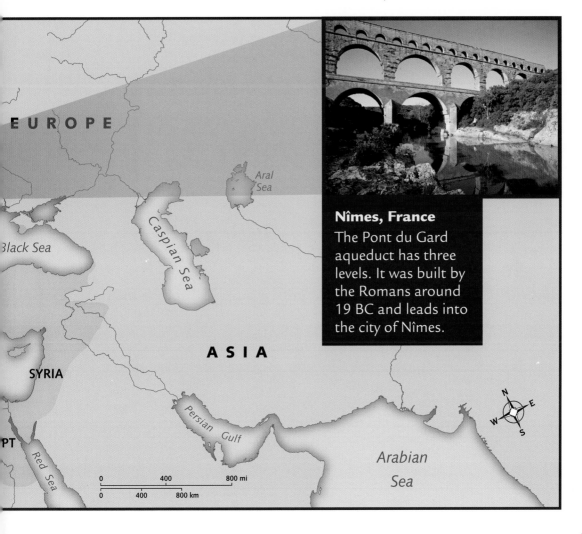

Nîmes, France
The Pont du Gard aqueduct has three levels. It was built by the Romans around 19 BC and leads into the city of Nîmes.

KEEP GOING!

Here are some ways to share what you've learned, find out more, and develop your talents. Maybe you'll come up with your own idea.

THINK AND WRITE

Imagine you recently moved to the ancient city of Rome from a farm in the country. Your cousin still lives back in the countryside, where no plumbing yet exists. Write a letter to your cousin describing all the fancy new water delivery systems, including the aqueducts, fountains, and baths. Explain what you think of them.

DIG DEEPER

What questions that you had before you read the book are still unanswered? What new questions came up in reading? You can start looking for answers in these Websites. Write down your answers and tell where you found them.

Nova Online: Secrets of Lost Empires: Roman Bath
www.pbs.org/wgbh/nova/lostempires/roman/

Bathing—The Roman Way
www.aclresources.net/romanbathsbathing/index.html

Odyssey Online—Rome
carlos.emory.edu/ODYSSEY/ROME/homepg.html

TALK TO THE EXPERTS

Use resources in your community or Websites to help you:

Read an interview with ancient Rome aqueduct expert Peter Aicher:
www.pbs.org/wgbh/nova/lostempires/roman/watering.html

Interview a professor of classics, architecture, or history at a local college. Ask him or her about the plumbing in ancient Rome and its effect on everyday life in the city.

DESIGN A ROMAN BATH

The year is AD 50, and you and your team of architects have been hired by the Roman emperor to design a public bath. Using the information and pictures in *Taking a Bath in Rome*, the Websites listed in the Dig Deeper box, and other on-line and print resources, work with a small group to create a plan. If you wish, use the plan to build an actual model. Share your work with the rest of the class.

GLOSSARY

apodyterium \ə pä də tir´ ē əm\ *n*. the changing room in a Roman bath

aqueduct \a´ kwə dəkt\ *n*. a channel used for carrying large amounts of flowing water

arch \ärch\ *n*. a curved design that makes the shape of an upside-down "u"

architecture \är´ kə tek chər\ *n*. the art or science of designing and building structures

barbarian \bär ber´ ē ən\ *n*. an invader from another land in ancient Roman times

bath \bath\ *n*. a building containing a series of rooms designed for bathing

caldarium \kal der´ ē əm\ *n*. the hottest room in an ancient Roman bath

cauldron \kôl´ drən\ *n*. a large kettle or boiler

channel \cha´ nəl\ *n*. a long gutter or groove that water can flow through

emperor \em´ pər ər\ *n*. the ruler of an empire

empire \em´ pīr\ *n*. a far-reaching group of lands or countries that are ruled by a single government

engineer \en jə nir´\ *n*. a person who is trained to build machines, roads, bridges, and other structures

filter \fil´ tər\ *v*. sift out

frigidarium \fri ji der´ ē əm\ *n*. the coldest room in an ancient Roman bath

gravity \gra´ və tē\ *n*. a physical force that pulls bodies and objects downward toward Earth

hypocaust \ hī´ pə kôst\ *n*. an ancient Roman central heating system with an underground furnace

latrine \lə trēn´\ *n*. a toilet

metropolis \mə trä´ pə ləs\ *n*. the chief city of a country or large area

mosaic \mō zā´ ik\ *n*. a decoration or picture made by putting together small pieces of different-colored materials to make shapes and patterns on a surface

natatorium \nā tə tor´ ē əm \ *n*. a swimming pool in an ancient Roman bath

palaestra \pə les´ trə\ *n*. an exercise yard in an ancient Roman bath

sewer \sü´ ər\ *n*. a channel for carrying waste and extra water out of a city

strigil \ stri´ jəl\ *n*. a long curved metal tool used for scraping dirt and oil off skin

tepidarium \te pi der´ ē əm\ *n*. a warm room in an ancient Roman bath

valve \valv\ *n*. device that can open or close a pipe

Pronunciation Key

\ə\ **a**mong \ər\ m**ur**der \a\ **a**sk \ā\ **a**pe \ä\ h**o**p, c**a**r \ch\ **ch**op \e\ **e**nd \ē\ gr**ea**sy \g\ **g**et
\i\ h**i**d \ī\ **i**ce \j\ **j**et \ŋ\ ki**ng** \ō\ n**o** \ô\ s**aw** \oi\ t**oy** \oo\ b**oo**k \ou\ **ou**t \th\ **th**ank \<u>th</u>\ **th**en
\ü\ b**oo**t \y\ **y**ou \zh\ A**s**ian

Index